HAPPY JAMMIN'
Really Cool Music for Recorders with Optional Barred-Percussion Ensemble

Paul Corbière

Editor: Jeanette Morgan
Cover Design: Jeff Richards
Book Design: WordStreamCopy

Permission-to-Reproduce Notice
Permission to photocopy the student scores in this product is hereby granted to one teacher as part of the purchase price. This permission may not be transferred, sold, or given to any additional or subsequent user of this product. Thank you for respecting the copyright laws.

© 2011 Heritage Music Press, a division of The Lorenz Corporation, and its licensors. All rights reserved.

Heritage Music Press
A division of The Lorenz Corporation
PO Box 802
Dayton OH 45401
www.lorenz.com

Printed in the United States of America.

ISBN: 978-1-4291-2698-4

HERITAGE MUSIC PRESS
A Lorenz Company • www.lorenz.com

Contents

	Page	CD Tracks Perf./Acc.
Preface	3	
Getting Started	4	
Sheet Music	4	
Performances	4	
Teaching the Pieces	5	
Instrument Substitutions	6	
Dix Ans (Ten Years)	7	1/11
Hidden Path	11	2/12
Wind Chime	15	3/13
No Worries	20	4/14
Gentle Rain	24	5/15
Five Jive	28	6/16
Cedar Falls	32	7/17
March	36	8/18
Coral	40	9/19
Meet the Composer	48	
Special Thanks	48	

About the Digital Files

The CD included in this product is enhanced and contains both audio tracks and digital files. The CD will play audio files like any regular CD in your CD player. To access the digital files, you will need a PDF reader, such as Adobe Reader, which you can download for free at http://get.adobe.com/reader/. Once you have installed Adobe Reader, simply insert your CD into your computer's CD drive. When prompted, click on **View Files** to see all of the resources available to you.

Preface

As a self-professed recorder geek, I've used a variety of different recorder methods with my students over the years. I discovered that when my students were playing the well-known tunes found in many recorder methods, they were rarely actually reading the notation. Instead, they were playing by ear and essentially figuring out how to play the pieces without knowing what notes they were playing or how to translate music on the page into what to play on the instrument. While playing songs by ear is a tremendously important skill—one that helps kids begin to understand the basics of improvisation—sight-reading is an equally important component of a quality general music program. I wrote the pieces in this book to ensure that my students would have to read the notation in order to play the music, and I wanted the songs to be interesting and fun to play so the kids would be motivated to do so. I have combined these pieces with drums and other percussion to encourage my students to work on their improvisation skills while helping them learn the skill of reading notation.

These pieces are unfamiliar to students and offer educators the opportunity to discuss sight-reading as a process, with a step-by-step procedure. Whenever you give your students a new piece of music, I suggest going through the following process:

1. Check the basics: time signature, key signature, repeat signs, and other "road map" indicators.

2. Examine rhythm patterns.

3. Examine melodic patterns.

4. Look for like phrases and repeated patterns.

5. Look for, and possibly work out in advance, any passage that may contain a new note or tricky note combination. Students' ability to play a difficult pattern at a steady tempo will contribute to their overall success.

6. Play the piece slowly; your students must teach their minds the correct fingering for each note they see. Speed is not important.

The goal in sight-reading is to play steadily and accurately. Your players may find this challenge daunting at first, but with perseverance they also may find a new joy in playing the recorder or any other instrument. The skill of sight-reading—examining what we know and what new information is being presented (problem solving)—is as beneficial to players when they are outside of the music realm as when they are seated in your classroom.

Enjoy the process!

Paul Corbière

Getting Started

Following are a few things you should consider before introducing any of these pieces to your students.

Sheet Music

These pieces combine two separate teaching styles: a sheet music-based approach *and* an oral-aural tradition.

I begin each piece by having everyone learn to play the recorder part from the sheet music. This is a key component of my teaching process. I *always* have the recorder part visible to my players when learning the music, even when I teach in a "my turn/your turn" style. I refer to the notation as they learn each piece. This fosters good music-reading skills.

The recorder parts are available in this text and on the accompanying CD as digital files. You may print and hand out copies or display them by using an LCD projector right from your computer.

> ! *The "Teaching Process" assumes that all of your students have worked on the recorder parts before you present the full ensemble. When you are introducing the ensemble, you should have to spend only a few minutes reviewing the recorder parts.*

Once the recorder parts are secure, I teach the percussion ensembles in an oral-aural tradition. I learned this teaching style by attending workshops on the World Music Drumming curriculum, written by Will Schmid and published by the Hal Leonard Corporation. (I haves subsequently become a staff member.) The students will not see the written parts for these instruments.

Performances

Staging is an important aspect to performances of all types. The correct placement of the instruments within the ensemble will help balance the sound. Here are a few tips to consider when staging these pieces:

- Create instrument sections: Low drums in one section, medium drums in another, and so on. Each section will be able to work together and if there are issues during a performance, the leader can address a section and easily fix the problem. Frequently, the problem fixes itself because of the teamwork necessary for playing this type of music.

- Contra bass bars should be at the front of the ensemble. Their sound and visual appeal will get lost if buried in the back of the group.

- Recorder players should be in a group and in front of the percussion instruments. I stage my recorder players off to the side, usually near a microphone. Refrain from instructing your students to try to play louder than the drums. They will lose this battle! Instead, encourage them to become a force within the ensemble and play together. Their combined sound will carry over the entire group.

Teaching the Pieces

Prepare for your teaching by reading through the entire lesson suggestions for a piece and understanding how the different parts fit together. Within the suggestions for each piece there are several sections, which are defined here.

Score Study: The "Score Study" section may refer to one or more parts of the ensemble as the *time line*. The time line is the musical leader of the ensemble and is frequently played with bells or claves. Every other part is based on its relationship to the time line. Understanding this relationship is the key to successful group playing and stresses the importance of the time line players' role in the group. As the group plays, the students may "tug and push" the beat or groove; the time line players must resist this and maintain a steady tempo.

While players must know their individual parts, they also need to know the relationship to the time line as well as to other parts in the ensemble. This encourages balance within the ensemble, as the players will inherently listen to each other more when they know how the piece is put together.

Sticking (which hand plays what for drums and xylophones) is another aspect of score study. Understanding the suggestions for sticking before attempting to teach any of this music is of utmost importance. Sticking suggestions are written with a right-handed person in mind (someone whose right hand is the stronger hand). Left-handed people should reverse the suggested sticking. As a result, each player should use his or her true dominant hand; the players should not mirror.

Teaching Process: In addition to listing a specific process, I may also identify potential problem spots in the music. Teach your students to attack these first; beginning students often do just the opposite. They practice what they can play easily and don't spend enough time on the more difficult passages. I also teach my players to look for patterns that repeat.

> *Work through the "Score Study" and "Teaching Process" sections, and study the actual score while teaching yourself the parts. Only then will you be ready to begin!* **!**

Performance Suggestions: In this section, I explain a plan for constructing each piece; this outline mirrors the recording on the CD. In general, layer in the parts. Never add a new part if the ensemble is not ready at that moment. Avoid predetermining when parts will come in, such as in every four beats (or measures). Instead, there should be a leader (you or a competent student) who determines the entrances of each part as the performance is taking place. Of course, these are only performance suggestions; the real fun is when a performing group creates its own unique versions.

Extensions: I may suggest other activities that could extend each ensemble for further study or additional effects, arrangements, and so on.

Small Ensemble: This section lists suggested instruments to use with a small ensemble.

Multiple Scores: I have provided scores for different levels of ensemble playing. There are small-ensemble scores for each recorder piece as well as full-ensemble scores. Some classrooms have Orff-style instruments and others have those and a complete complement of drums. Some classrooms may have only recorders and nothing else. The multiple scores for each piece provide a variety of options to allow any classroom to play these pieces successfully. Be sure to look in the digital files to see all the versions of each piece.

Instrument Substitutions

Do not feel like you must use the instruments I have listed on the scores. I often teach the recorder part with my Hohner melodica for two reasons:

1. It's fun!
2. My players must learn the notes to play—not watch my fingers!

Here are some more ways in which you can adapt instruments:

- Recorders can be replaced with any C instrument.
- High drum parts can be played by bongos, children's tom-toms, or small, high-pitched frame drums.
- Low and medium drums can be played by congas or low-sounding drums.
- Gankogui (African double bells) can be replaced with cowbells or other metal bells.
- Contra bass bar parts can be played by a bass guitar or a keyboard instrument.
- Shekeres, rattles, or maracas can be replaced with any type of shakers.

Dix Ans

Ten years

This piece was written to commemorate the ten-year anniversary of the Beat for Peace drumming program, which started in 1999 at Starlight Cove Elementary School in Lantana, Florida.

Yes, this is a B, A, G piece! I have included it in this collection as an easy introductory piece to help students become familiar with combining an entire ensemble (drums, percussion, Orff-style instruments, and so on) with recorders. This can be overwhelming at first. Follow the process below and remember that repetition is our friend; don't be afraid to repeat parts or phrases until the ensemble is playing each part correctly and together.

Grades: 3–4

Pitches: G, A, B

Small Ensemble

- Claves
- Low drum
- Alto xylophone
- Bass xylophone

Small-ensemble scores are available as digital files on the CD.

Score Study

- The claves are the time line.
- Look at the recorder part and note its relationship to the time line.
- Note the relationship between the low drum part and the time line.
- Observe that the shekere and high drum parts play on the same beat.
- When studying the xylophone parts, notice that both parts share beat 4. The low drum part also shares this groove.

Teaching Process

1. Teach the claves (time line) part to everyone. Have your students clap this rhythm until they all can perform it steadily and consistently.

2. The recorder players should review B, A, and G fingerings. Distribute the recorder music and review the recorder parts. Be sure that the students observe and count the rests. This will help them maintain the beat in the second recorder part.

3. Combine the claves with the recorder ensemble to help keep a steady beat. Continue to have the claves play when learning and reviewing the recorder parts because they share the same rhythmic motif.

4. Next, teach the low drum part. Fit it to the time line (the first two notes of the low drum part play with the time line).

5. Teach the shekere and high drum parts. These players should look at each other when they play.

6. Teach the bass xylophone, then the alto xylophone parts. Be sure they play the fourth beat together.

7. Teach the medium drum part using the suggested sticking.

Performance Suggestions

- Layer in all the parts in the following order: claves, shekere, low drums, medium drums, high drums, bass xylophones, alto xylophones, recorder 1, and recorder 2 parts.

Extensions

- During the interludes, the recorder players can perform a number of movement activities, such as a circle dance or creative movement with their recorders. My students like to take out flags or streamers and do synchronized movements.

- Instead of playing the recorder 2 part, players may improvise during the four-beat breaks on a variety of instruments (including recorders).

Dix Ans
Ten Years

Paul Corbière

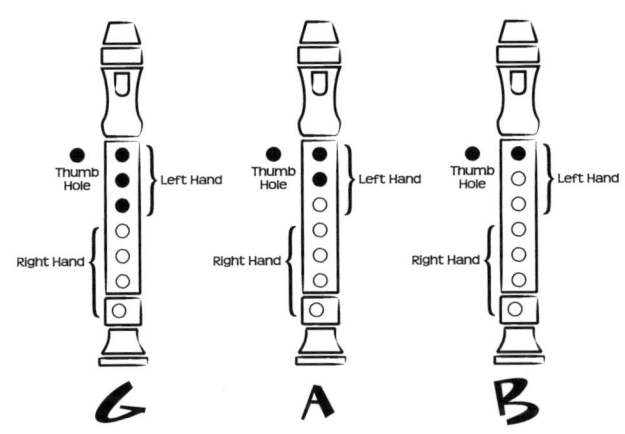

Dix Ans
Ten Years

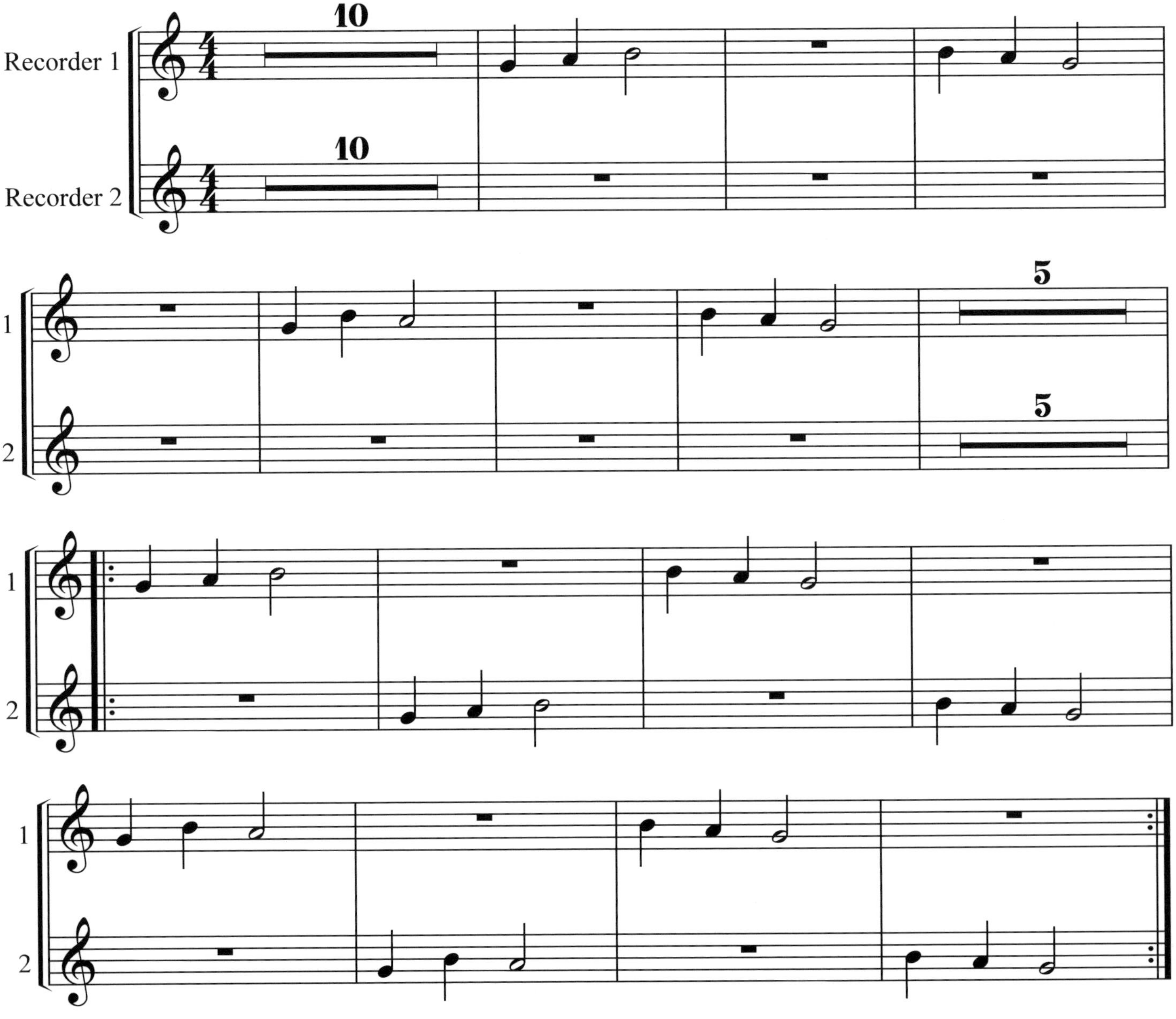

Paul Corbière

Hidden Path

"Hidden Path" uses both low D and low E on the recorder. The melody contains step, skip, and leap motions. You can examine all of these elements in the recorder score. Take this as an opportunity to review these concepts.

Grades: 3–4

Pitches: D, E, G, A, B

Small Ensemble

Option 1	Option 2
• Claves	• Claves
• Triangle	• Medium drum
• Medium drum	• Metallophone
• Glockenspiel	Small-ensemble scores are available as digital files on the CD.
• Metallophone	
• Bass xylophone	

Score Study

- The claves are the time line.
- Look at the recorder part and notice its relationship to the time line.
- Note the relationship of the glockenspiel and bass xylophone parts to each other and to the time line.
- Note the shekere part's relationship to the time line. The medium drum has a similar complementary part in relationship to the time line.

Teaching Process

1. First, teach the claves to everyone. Have your students clap this rhythm until they can perform it steadily and consistently.
2. Review the fingers for pitches D, E, G, A, and B on the recorders. Hand out the recorder music and review the recorder part.
3. Combine the claves with the recorder ensemble to help keep a steady beat. Continue to have the claves play when learning and reviewing the recorder part. This teaches your players to regard the time line as the leader of the ensemble.
4. Teach the xylophone parts (bass, then alto). Add these parts to the ensemble.
5. Once the claves, recorder, and xylophone parts are solid, introduce all of the other instrumental parts, one at a time.

Performance Suggestions

1. Begin with a solo (unaccompanied) recorder player, playing the first eight measures of their melody.

2. After a brief pause, the claves play one measure of their part on their own.

3. Layer in the triangle, temple block, alto metallophone, shekere, bass xylophone, and alto xylophone parts.

4. The recorders (all players) play the entire melody with the instruments as listed in the previous step. The recorders drop out; the other instruments continue.

5. Layer in the glockenspiel, medium drum, low drum, and high drum parts.

6. The recorders reenter and play the entire melody in unison, then break into a two-part round (see the recorder music for details), with each recorder playing the melody twice.

7. After the recorders complete the round, end the piece by fading out the rest of the ensemble.

Extensions

- Experiment with the recorder round: it could be a two-, three-, or four-part round. Guide your students to discover where to place the entrances, trying different entry points. Challenge your students to explore the possibility that other parts could be played as a round.

- Incorporate alto or tenor recorders playing the glockenspiel part as a countermelody to the soprano recorder part. Hint: This can become a round as well!

- Interval study: Examine the recorder part and have your players describe the melodic movement as it moves by steps, skips, leaps, and repeated tones.

Hidden Path

Paul Corbière

Wind Chime

"Wind Chime" is a favorite piece for my players, despite some of the challenges they must tackle. Counting rests, specifically the whole and half rests, became a problem for my players. This was not because they had to count two or four beats of silence, but because of the duration of the notes prior to the rests. This piece forced my players to play a whole note for four beats only and not hang on to it longer. Becoming intensely aware of these details has transformed my players into better listeners. Better listening has translated to an increase in the group's musicianship.

Grades: 4–6

Pitches: D, E, G, A, B

Small Ensemble

- Claves
- Temple block*
- Triangle
- Metallophone 1

Small-ensemble scores are available as digital files on the CD.

There is a three-mallet part for one of the metallophone players. This a great challenge for a more advanced player.

"Wind Chime" also allows further study of the dotted quarter and eighth note combination. In my classroom, most of our practicing was dedicated to the accuracy of this rhythm. The recorder part itself is not difficult, provided your students know D, E, G, A, and B.

* You may substitute a low-sounding wood block if you do not have a set of temple blocks.

  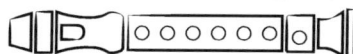

Score Study

- The time line in "Wind Chime" is created by the combination of the claves, temple block, and triangle parts. Study these parts carefully to understand how they interact and create a cohesive time line rhythm.

- Study the sticking for the medium drum part. The "x" notes are muted tones and should be performed using the fingertips of both hands hitting in the center of the drum (beat 3). It is a time-keeping stroke and should be barely audible.

- The low drum part contains a slap (x), an advanced technique for hand drumming. If your players know this technique, there should be no problem adding it. If you are unsure of this technique, see the "Teaching Process" section for instructions for creating a "cheating" slap.

Teaching Process

1. Teach the time line part to its respective instruments in this order: claves, triangle, temple blocks. Be sure to teach the time line to all of your students, using vocalizations or body percussion for the students who are not assigned to time line instruments.

2. Practice the time line until the kids can play it steadily for a sustained period of time.

3. Review the fingerings for pitches D, E, G, A, and B. Review the recorder parts.

4. Teach the metallophone parts. The metallophone 1 part proves to be the biggest challenge because of the dotted quarter and eighth note rhythm. Teach your players to use proper counting (1, 2 *and* 3, 4; 1 ...).

> ! *Be sure to show your recorder players how the E on beat 1 of the second measure of the metallophone 1 part is the starting point for the recorder part. Explain that they can use the E as a marker at which point they should release the long tones and prepare for the two half rests in their part.*

Metallophone 2 begins when metallophone 1 plays the E. Once this part begins, the players can take their cue from the time line for the rest of the piece. Metallophone 3 employs a three-mallet technique. I suggest having two mallets in the right hand. Place the two mallets in the right hand with the inside, or left, mallet under the other in the palm of the hand. Extend the index finger between the mallets to create the proper interval needed, in this case a third, and allow the rest of the hand to wrap comfortably around the mallets. The notes played by this hand do not change.

5. Now move to the drums! As you teach the drum parts, have students perform each part with the time line. Knowing the relationship of the part to the time line is crucial to holding a steady beat and not rushing the tempo. Keep the time line going when teaching each drum part. Teach the low drum part first. There are many ways to achieve the slap on the drum, all of which take a lot of time and patience. If your players are not familiar with the slap technique, you may suggest that these players open one hand (fingers spread), leave the hand on the drumhead for the slapped note, and keep the hand closed (fingers together) coming off the drumhead for the regular tones. The slap is hit on the drum where the high tones are placed. Next, teach the high drum part. Use an alternating hand pattern and notice how it fills in the low drum part on beat 3 to beat 4. Finally, teach the medium drum part. There is a suggested sticking for this part, but remember that some players may perform the sticking pattern opposite (leading with the left hand).

Performance Suggestions

Layer in the parts in this order:

1. Begin with the claves, the temple blocks, and the triangle.
2. Play each of the metallophone parts as written in the score with the time line parts still playing.
3. Layer in the drum parts (low, medium, and then high drum).
4. Layer in metallophone 1. The recorders play the melody as metallophone 1 plays.
5. After the recorder melody, metallophone 2 joins metallophone 1.
6. The recorders play the melody with the non-pitched percussion and metallophones 1 and 2.
7. After the recorder melody, metallophone 3 joins in with metallophones 1 and 2 and continues as the recorder melody plays again.
8. Fade out the ending.

Do not play this piece too fast! (The drums usually want to rush it.) **!**

Extensions

- When performing "Wind Chime," I add wind chimes as a color instrument to the performance. My players begin playing them very softly and intermittently before the metallophones enter. Students then play the three metallophone parts *out of time* to give the audience the sensation of hearing a real set of wind chimes. By *out of time*, I mean that the part is rhythmically free but the tones are in the right order. Then I ask my players to play their individual parts correctly. For the best effect, do not play these three parts at the same time during the introduction; this allows for your audience to hear these parts by themselves. Then, layer in the claves, the temple blocks, the triangle, and the rest of the ensemble. Begin the metallophone 1 part, and as the other parts enter, allow the wind chimes to fade out.

- I also use wind chimes at the ending and allow them to take over the metallophone parts as the three parts slow and play out of time—a technique that I describe as *letting the parts break down*. My players understand this expression because we have played other pieces that do this same thing. It really helps everything to just fade away. The drum and rhythm parts fade out while maintaining rhythmic accuracy as the wind chimes take over. My players love his effect because it never sounds the same when we perform the piece.

Wind Chime

Paul Corbière

x = muted tone; fingertips from both hands touch in center of drum and should be very soft
(x) = slap

Verse 2
I sing too, hearing the sweet sound.
Sweetly calling me, all around.

Verse 3
Shimm'ring sounds are floating by me.
Calming spirits, peacefully.

The original purchaser of *Happy Jammin'* (30/2758H) by Paul Corbière has permission to reproduce this page for use in his/her classroom. © 2011 Heritage Music Press, a division of The Lorenz Corporation, and its licensors. All rights reserved.

No Worries

PERF. ACC.
4 · 14

This piece introduces high D to your recorder players. The tempo is not fast, so use this to your advantage and discuss intonation and blending. Be sure to encourage your recorder players to listen to each other and blend.

Grades: 3–4

Pitches: E, G, A, B, high D

Small Ensemble
- Claves
- Shekere
- Low drum
- Alto xylophone
- Bass xylophone

  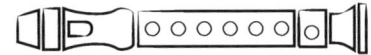

Score Study
- The bell begins the piece as the time line; the claves part takes over as the time line at measure 2 and is the part on which your recorder players will rely.
- Note the similarity of the low drum and alto xylophone parts.
- Observe the sticking pattern for the low drum part.
- Look at the medium drum part and note the slap tone.
- Notice the relationship between the shekere and bass xylophone parts; the high drum part also has a similar rhythm.
- The shekere rhythm is central to the groove of the entire piece.

Teaching Process
1. Start with the recorders. Review the fingering for high D. Practice sustaining this note while producing an even tone, and listening to and playing in tune with each other.

! *Suggest that your students use smooth, warm air.*

Divide the recorder players into two groups and play the harmonies from the score (B and high D, B and G, A and E). Practice holding these tones and listening to the blended sounds before moving on to reading the music. Hand out the recorder scores and review them together.

2. Teach the claves part.

3. Teach the shekere part. For a crisper sound, a student should place the shekere in both hands and play the rhythm by tapping his or her fingers on the bottom of the instrument.

4. Teach the bass xylophone part, noting the relationship of the bass xylophone and shekere parts.

5. Teach the bell, low drum, and alto xylophone parts.

6. Teach the high drum and medium drum parts.

7. Finally, combine all parts of the ensemble.

Performance Suggestions

1. Layer in the parts in this order: bell, shekere, claves, high drum, medium drum, low drum, alto xylophone, and bass xylophone.

2. Recorder 1 plays.

3. After the recorder melody, all instruments drop out except the shekere. The shekere plays through its part one time and then all instruments (except the recorders) come back.

4. Recorders 1 and 2 return and play the melody.

5. Repeat the melody and fade out.

Extensions

- To maximize the recorders' harmonic impact, have the bass xylophones play only the low E the first time through the recorder melody. After the shekere interlude, add the B to the part.

- Add a metallophone or "clean-sounding" electric guitar on the melody.

No Worries

Paul Corbière

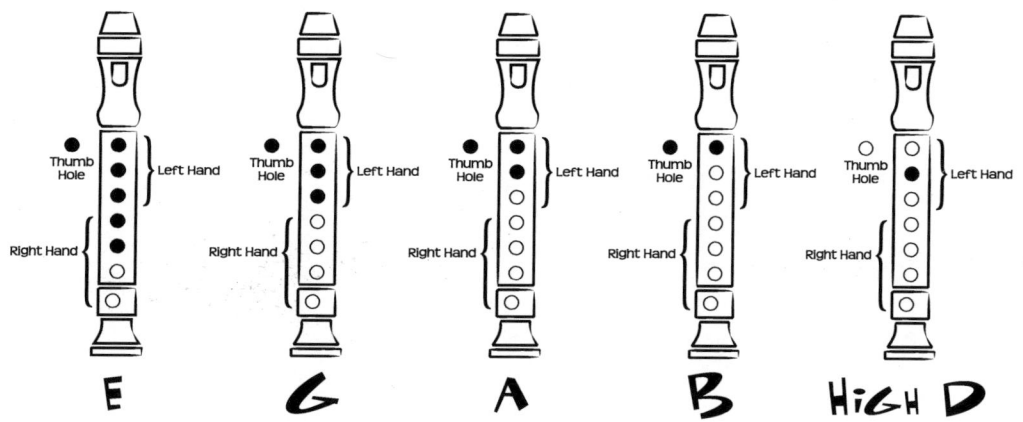

No Worries

Paul Corbière

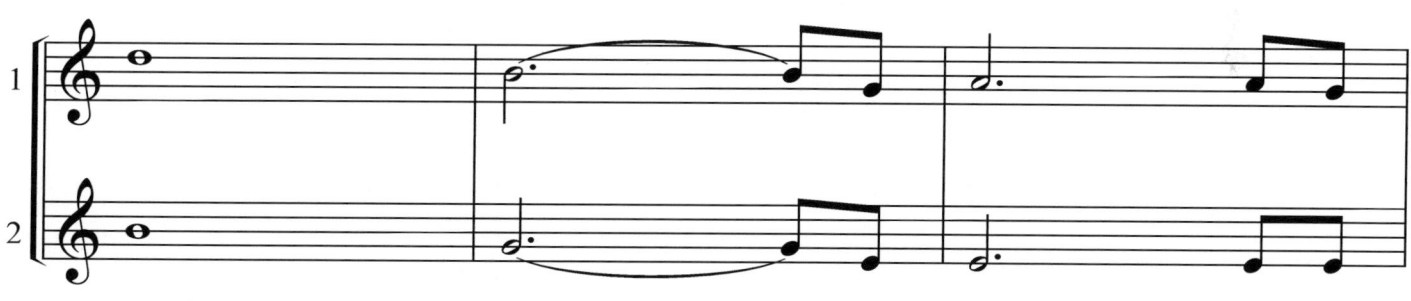

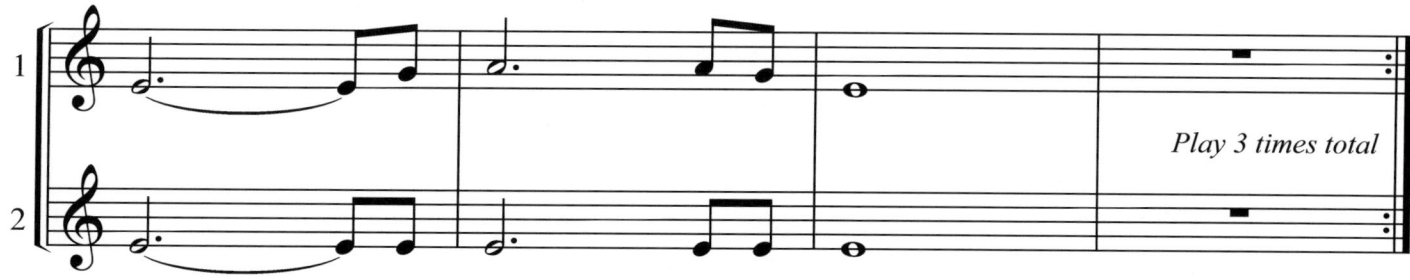

Gentle Rain

PERF. ACC.

"Gentle Rain" introduces high E to your players, expanding their note-playing range to an octave. "Gentle Rain" is also the first piece in this book with articulation notated in the recorder part. Explore the *staccato* markings (rain drops) and work on playing both *staccato* and *legato*. Taking the time for these details shows your players your expectation of fine musicianship.

Grades: 5–6

Pitches: E, G, A, B, high C, high D, high E

Small Ensemble

- Temple block
- Triangle
- Frog rasp
- Low drum
- Metallophone
- Alto xylophone
- Bass xylophone

Score Study

- The temple block part is the time line.
- Note the recorder part. The first and third phrases are identical; the second and fourth begin the same, but end differently.
- The drum parts are played with mallets. Frame drums (with various high and low pitches) can be substituted. I suggest using felt mallets for the best sound.
- Remove the F and B xylophone bars to help players perform the downward patterns accurately.

Teaching Process

1. Teach the temple block part first.
2. Teach each drum part separately, noting how each part fits with the time line.
3. Combine all of the drums together with the time line.
4. Teach each xylophone part separately, noting its relationship to the time line.
5. Review all the notes for the recorder part.
6. Review the recorder part and play through it a few times; don't forget the articulations.

> *My players find it easier to produce the high E by pushing their thumbnail into the thumbhole on the back of the recorder, rather than trying to cover half the hole with the pad of their thumb.*

Performance Suggestions

1. We use rainsticks, an ocean drum, a mark tree, and other various sounds to create an improvised introduction. Choose sounds that shimmer (finger cymbals, different metal objects ... ringing sounds). From this texture, the temple block part emerges, followed by rest of the instruments.

2. Layer in the parts in this order: low drum, medium drum, high drum, metallophone, and bass xylophone.

3. Play the recorder melody.

4. Add the alto xylophone part.

5. Play the recorder melody again.

6. Fade out the ending and add the sounds from the introduction as a coda.

Extensions

- Think about creating the mood of this piece. Ask, "What would music sound like in a gentle rain?" Discuss the importance of mood in music. Allow your players to experiment with various pitched and non-pitched instruments to create a mood for this piece. Vocabulary may include words such as *calm*, *peaceful*, *still*, *gentle*, and *somber*.

- Discuss the playful mood of the recorder melody and the juxtaposition of this seemingly happy recorder part and a gentle rain.

- When my ensemble plays this piece, we create a little rainstorm to introduce the piece. (See the first step under Performance Suggestions.)

Gentle Rain

Paul Corbière

Five Jive

"Five Jive" is a fun piece with a cool factor of ten! Of course, telling players that the time signature of $\frac{5}{4}$ is very difficult to play is not recommended. In fact, with the proper score study on your part, they won't know that it is challenging at all and will be very successful.

Grades: 5–6

Pitches: E, G, A, B, high D, high E

Small Ensemble

- Shekere
- Low drum
- Metallophone
- Alto xylophone
- Bass xylophone

Score Study

- The shekere part is the time line.
- The pattern is felt as a three-beat pattern followed by a two-beat pattern. To clarify, each measure will feel like 1, 2, 3, 1, 2.
- The gankogui and shekere parts share their first two notes. Being aware of this relationship will keep the parts together.

Teaching Process

1. Prepare for the recorder part by reviewing the fingerings for E, G, A, B, high D, and high E. Practice the melodic movement in the recorder part: B to high D to B; B to high E to A. Play each note with long tones to isolate the fingerings. Hand out the music and review the recorder part.

2. Teach the shekere and metallophone parts separately. Have the recorders listen to these instruments to feel the 3 against 2 subdivision.

3. Teach the three xylophone parts. The relationship between these parts will help your players learn them very quickly. Note that beats 4 and 5 are played together.

4. Teach the low, medium, and high drum parts.

5. Teach the gankogui part. While this is the first part to be heard in the recording, I choose to teach it last because it may be difficult for younger players to master. This part drives the piece! However, if your players are struggling, you can leave it out. It can always be added later.

Remember, as the leader of your ensemble, you always have the right to leave out a part that your players cannot play or keep in time.

Performance Suggestions

1. Layer in the percussion parts in this order: gankogui, shekere, contra bass bar, bass xylophones, low drum, medium drum, alto xylophone, high drum, and metallophone.

2. Once all the parts are layered in, add the recorder melody.

3. The arrangement on the CD contains a four-measure interlude that is a unison rhythm played by everyone except the recorder players. The rhythmic pattern is:

Mallet instruments can choose any two notes from an E-minor chord to play as double-stops.

4. After this interlude, all parts come back in and play for four measures.

5. The recorder melody plays two times.

6. End with the group fading out.

Extension

- Included on the CD is a score for a version of "Five Jive" called "Five Jive (in Four)." The piece is rewritten in 4/4 time. Although one beat is taken away from each part, I tried to maintain the essence of the original.

- Learning and playing the alternate version may provide an opportunity for you and your players to demonstrate the idea of variation at a concert or an *informance*—that is, a performance that shares information regarding the processes and outcomes for musical study.

Five Jive

Paul Corbière

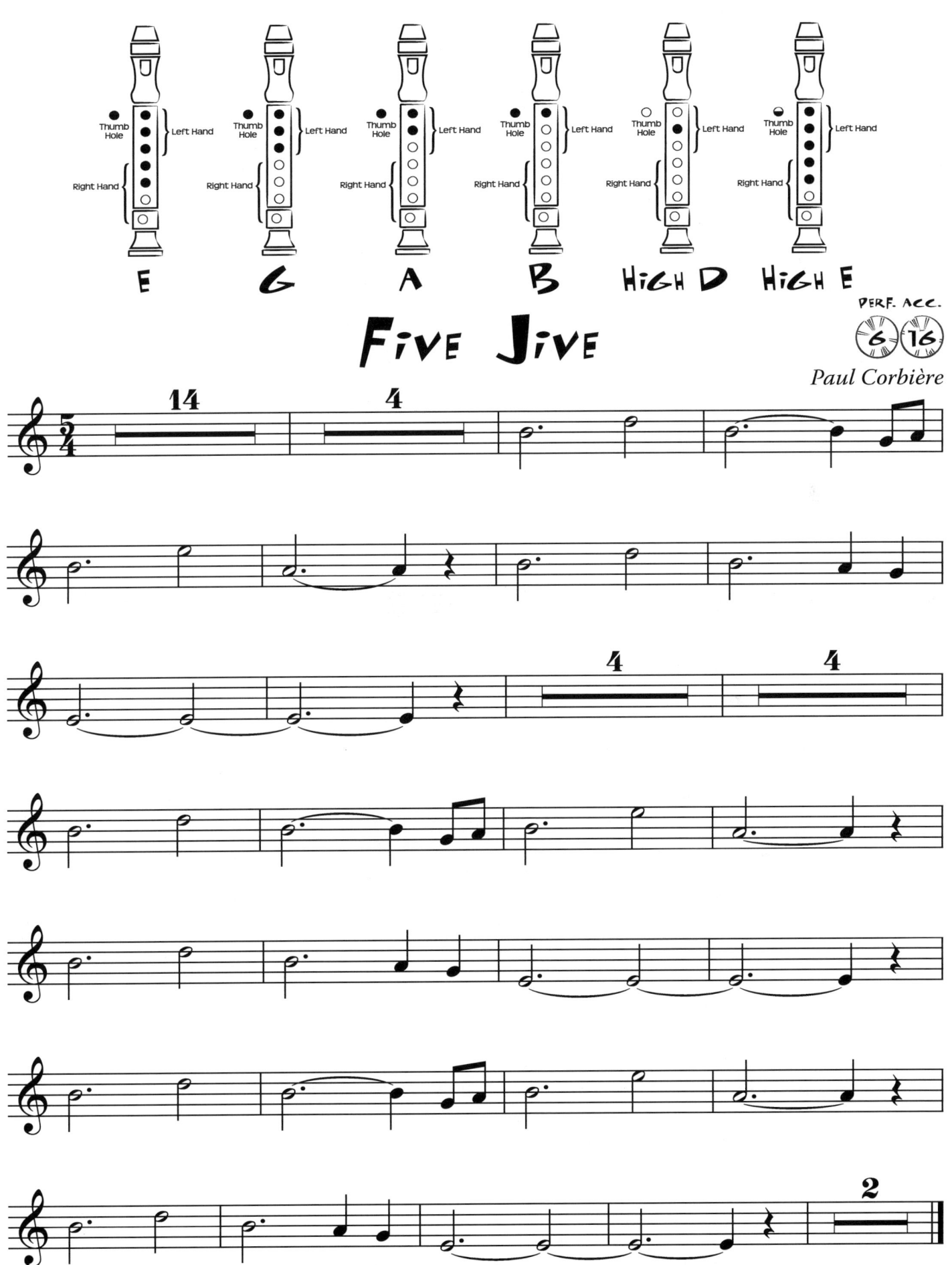

Cedar Falls

"Cedar Falls" is in 3/4 time and has a dancelike quality to it. After originally writing it in the key of F, I rewrote it in the key of G because it is an easier key for the recorders to play in. However, the full score and recorder part for the F version is included on the CD.

PERF. ACC. 7 17

Grades: 5–6

In the key of G: D, G, A, B, high C, high D

In the key of F: C, F, G, A, B-flat, high C

Small Ensemble

- Claves
- High drum
- Metallophone
- Alto xylophone
- Bass xylophone

Small-ensemble scores are available as digital files on the CD.

Score Study

- The claves part is the time line.
- The shekere and clave parts create a two-against-three pattern.
- The soprano metallophone part shares the same rhythm as the shekere part.
- The soprano and alto xylophones play double-stops, or two notes played simultaneously. This can be tricky, so practice these parts slowly, working on hitting both bars at exactly the same time.

Teaching Process

1. Teach the claves part (time line) by having all your students clap the part. Be sure to encourage your players to feel the beat in sets of three.

2. Teach the shekere part. For this part, your players must feel the beat in sets of two.

3. Teach the soprano and alto xylophone parts by playing only beat 1 of each measure. This will help solidify the chord changes and provide practice for the double-stops. Remind your players to hit both bars at the same time. Combine these parts with the time line (claves). Teach the rest of the part as written. The last eighth note of each measure is played with the left hand, followed by the double-stop on beat 1 of the next measure played by the right hand. This part can present challenges for your players. Practice slowly.

4. Teach the bass xylophone part and contra bass bar part.

5. Teach the alto metallophone part.

6. Teach the three drum parts. Start with the high drum part, then the medium and low drum parts together. When these parts are combined, the drum parts create a flowing pattern that gives the impression of a waterfall. Remind your drummers to play evenly with no accents.

7. Teach the soprano metallophone part. Remind the players to listen for the shekere part.

8. Review the fingerings for the recorder part. Distribute the music and review the recorder part.

Performance Suggestions

1. Layer in the parts in this order: claves, high drum, shekere, low drum, contra bass bar and bass xylophone, alto xylophone, soprano xylophone, medium drum, and alto metallophone.

2. Then the recorder plays through the melody once.

3. Add the soprano metallophone part during the interlude.

4. After the eight-bar interlude, the recorder part plays again.

5. Perform the eight-bar interlude again.

6. The recorder melody plays one more time to the end of the piece.

Extensions

- For an added challenge, print "Cedar Falls" in the key F from the CD and have a discussion with your players about performing the piece in a different key signature.

- Perform both versions and discuss which version they like better. This may lead to further discussion about melodies played in different keys. For example, the "Birthday Song" is never sung in the same key, but once a key is established, everyone can sing the song because the shape and the contour of the melody are the same in any key signature.

Cedar Falls

Paul Corbière

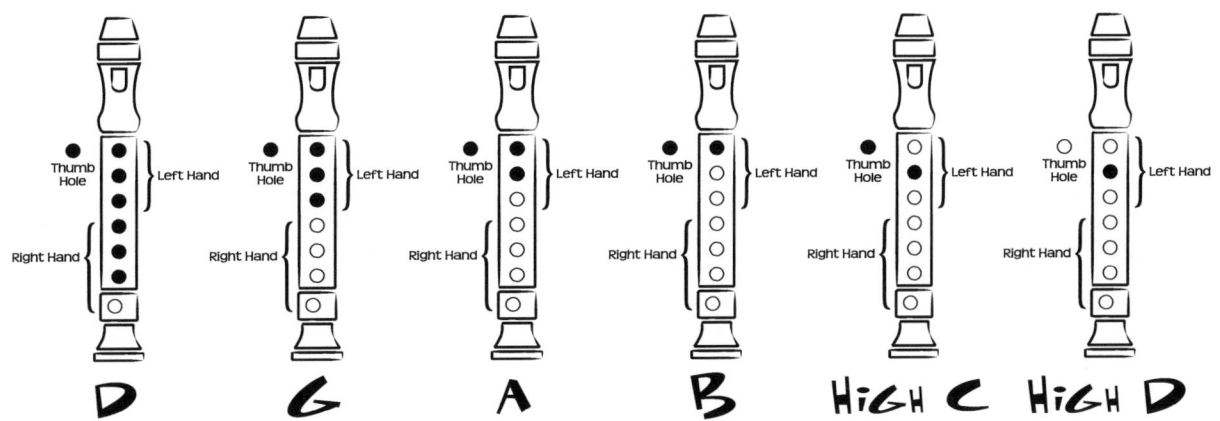

Cedar Falls

Paul Corbière

Play 3 times total

March

I wrote "March" to introduce F-sharp to my players. As they learned it, I realized that my players were adding articulations to the part. I have written them into the part and like the result of their suggestions.

Grades: 4–6

Pitches: D, F-sharp, G, A, B, high C

Small Ensemble
- Bell
- Shekere
- High drum*
- Frame drum
- Alto xylophone
- Bass xylophone

* In the small-ensemble score, the high drum part has been modified to be easier to play. You may choose to play the original part if you have students who can play it. It should be played on a higher-pitched drum. Bongos would be an excellent choice.

Score Study

- The bell part is the time line.
- The shekere part plays a supportive role throughout the ensemble.
- The medium drum and bass xylophone parts play identical rhythm patterns.
- There are four phrases in the recorder's melody; phrases 1, 2, and 3 are identical.

Teaching Process

1. Teach the bell part to everyone. This rhythm pattern is a two-beat followed by three-beat claves pattern. Get your players up and moving to a steady beat played on a shekere, if you wish. Then clap the bell pattern while moving (walking, stamping, etc.) to internalize the part.

2. Teach the maracas part. I suggest an alternating pattern such as the following:

    R–LR–L–RL–R–LR–L–RL–R

    Combine the maracas with the bell and the shekere parts.

3. Teach the alto xylophone and contra bass bar parts. Point out that these two parts are rhythmically similar to the shekere part.

4. Teach the frame drum and low drum parts. Keep the muted tones as soft as possible.

5. Teach the medium drum part with the bass xylophone part. They have the same rhythm. Play the low tones of the medium drum with the strong hand.

6. Teach the high drum part.

7. Review the fingerings for D, F-sharp, G, A, B, and high C with your recorder players. Prepare your students for the two difficult spots in the melody. They are the motifs found in measures 1 and 7. Practice these passages by slowly moving back and forth through each note change. Then shorten the length of each tone until the rhythm of this motif is played slowly. Once players can play the passage with comfort, hand out the recorder scores. Show your students that the melody begins on beat 2. Have the players practice saying "one" before they come in. My players like to stomp a foot on beat 1 so they can feel the entrance. Review the melody, being sure that students are playing the articulation that is notated.

8. Put the whole piece together for performance.

Performance Suggestions

1. Layer in the parts in this order: bell, shekere, maracas, contra bass bar, medium drum, bass xylophone, low drum, frame drum, alto xylophone, and high drum.

2. Once all the parts are in, add the recorder melody.

3. After the recorder melody plays, create an interlude section for improvisation.

4. After the improvisation, play the recorder melody two times and then fade out the ensemble to the end.

Extensions

- The maracas part can also be played by a small shekere. Substitute the right maraca with a downstroke on the shekere (on the knee) and the left with an upstroke (hitting the other hand).

- Substitute a snare drum for the high drum part and add a crash cymbal on beat 1 of each phrase of the recorder melody. This will amp up the piece, sounding like a real march!

March

Paul Corbière

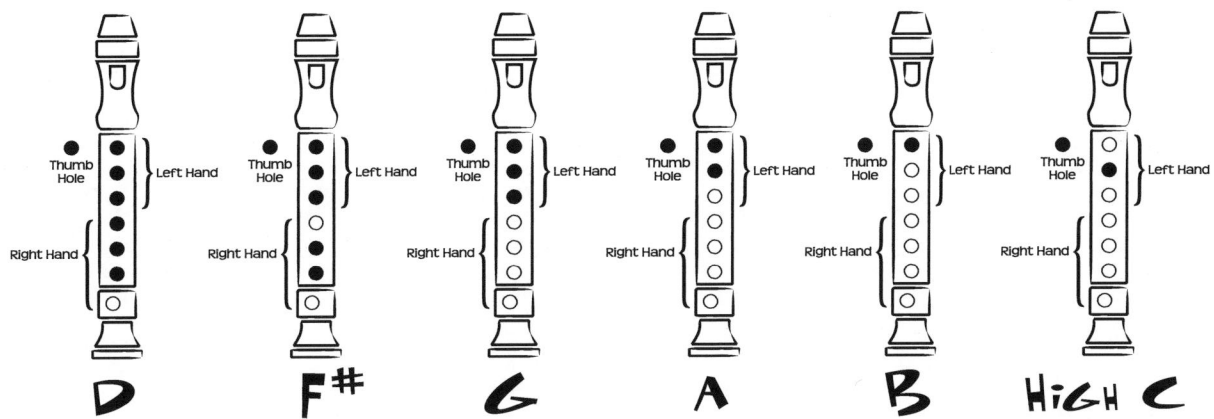

March

Paul Corbière

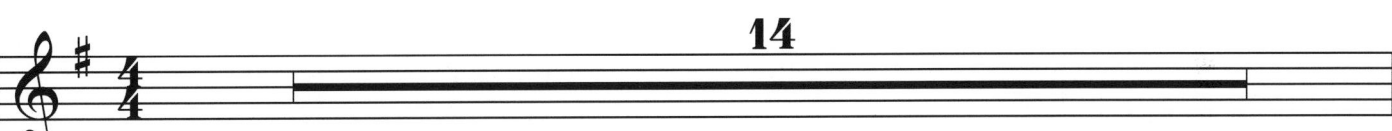

Play 3 times total

Coral

"Coral" was commissioned for the percussion group Shere Khan and was first performed by the group at the 2010 Children's Art Festival in Cape Girardeau, Missouri.

"Coral" explores a two-against-three polyrhythmic feel. This rhythmic idea is first set up by the time line (claves part) and the shekere part. The high bell and gankogui parts are optional and may provide for an interesting interlude between each statement (repeat) of the recorder part.

Grades: 5–6

Pitches: E, G, A, B, high C, high D

Small Ensemble

- Claves
- Shekere
- Medium drum

You may also use the bass xylophone and/or alto xylophone parts. I combined the three drum parts into one part for the small-ensemble arrangement. If it proves to be too much for your players, try using the original medium drum part from the full score.

Score Study

- The claves part is the time line. Its rhythm can be thought of as 1, 2; 1, 2, 3.
- The shekere part is written as a compound duple pattern.
- The contra bass bar part has the same rhythm as the time line.
- The alto and bass xylophone part is composed of two chords (E-minor and D-minor) that switch back and forth in the pattern sets of four, then two, with a final E-minor chord to end the piece.
- The high tones that each of the three drum parts play combine to create the drum melody.

Teaching Process

1. Teach the shekere part first. Have your players all stand and walk to this rhythm.

2. Teach the claves part. First, clap the rhythm of the part while walking to a steady beat. Choose students to play the shekere and the claves parts. Spend a lot of time on this activity, as it will enforce the two-against-three rhythm that drives this piece.

3. After teaching the time line, review the concept of subdividing. Subdividing this part yields the high bell part. I have my players count 1, 2, 3, 1, 2, 3; 1, 2, 1, 2, 1, 2. Another option may be 1 *and a* 2 *and a*; 1 *and* 2 *and* 3 *and*. Clap on beat 1 and say the subdivisions out loud. Remember that each of these subdivisions is played with the same pulse: the eighth note. Teach this as a group lesson so the entire group will be able to perform either part and gain a deeper understanding of this complementary relationship.

4. Teach the three drum parts. The drum melody consists of the high tones of each part. This is the composite rhythm:

    The notes that the high and low drums play that are marked with an "x" serve as timekeepers or place markers to help the players perform the part smoothly. The notes should be played softly. Have your students play the three drum parts slowly while you listen carefully. If all of the tones are played accurately, you should hear the composite rhythm (drum melody). This rhythm should not be taught to the students; it is for you to hear.

5. Teach the alto and bass xylophone part. Begin by teaching the following sticking for the part: L–R–L–R–L–R on any tones (low E and B are good choices). Then, once they can play this pattern evenly—with no accents—teach the E-minor chord from the score. Next, demonstrate how to *slide* to the next chord. I teach my players that *sliding* means playing one pattern of notes and then sliding the same rhythmic pattern onto a set of different tones. This change in the pattern is simple and your players will love the harmony it produces (since most things we hear are in a major key). Have the students practice sliding, on your command, back and forth between the E-minor and D-minor chords. Once they can accomplish this, give them the following pattern: 4 Es, 4 Ds, 4 Es, 4 Ds; then 2 Es, 2 Ds, 2 Ds, 2 Ds; then 1 E. I tell my players that this is a *holding pattern*, which is like a vamp: hanging out on a tonality until the melody begins and then following the pattern or chord progression above. Performing the same rhythmic or melodic patterns on various starting pitches allows players to experiment with improvisation.

6. Review the fingerings and pitches with your recorder players. Hand out the music and review the piece.

7. Now put it all together. Remember to add new instruments only when the ensemble is ready for them. Start with the time line and add layers in as suggested in the following section.

Performance Suggestions

1. Layer in the claves, shekere, gankogui, high bell, medium drum, high drum, and low drum parts.

2. Layer in the bass xylophone and alto xylophone part. Xylophones hold the E-minor tonality until the recorder melody starts; then they play the chord progression as notated.

3. Add the claves part and remove both bells.

4. Begin the recorder melody; begin the chord progression.

5. Create an interlude for improvisation.

6. Play the recorder melody.

7. Fade to the end.

> **!** *When we play "Coral" as a drums-only ensemble, I add the gankogui part (the subdivided bell part) to the bell part to create a more intricate time line.*

Extensions

- "Coral" was inspired by my love of snorkeling in the Florida Keys. As I was writing, I recalled my sense of peace as I floated on top of the water with all that life and activity moving below. The recorder part represents the snorkeler, who is calmly floating, observing all of the activity below: sea fans and other plant life swaying back and forth while all types and sizes of fish dart in and out of all of the plant and coral formations.

- Encourage your players to research the coral reefs that cover our planet. There are several videos available for free on the Internet that will show the beautiful nature of the reefs.

- Work with your players to add other sounds to "Coral" to simulate ocean and water sounds to enhance their performance.

- An additional extended performance track of "Coral" is provided on the CD. This version demonstrates one of the many ways that this (and all of the pieces in this collection) may be modified.

Coral

Paul Corbière

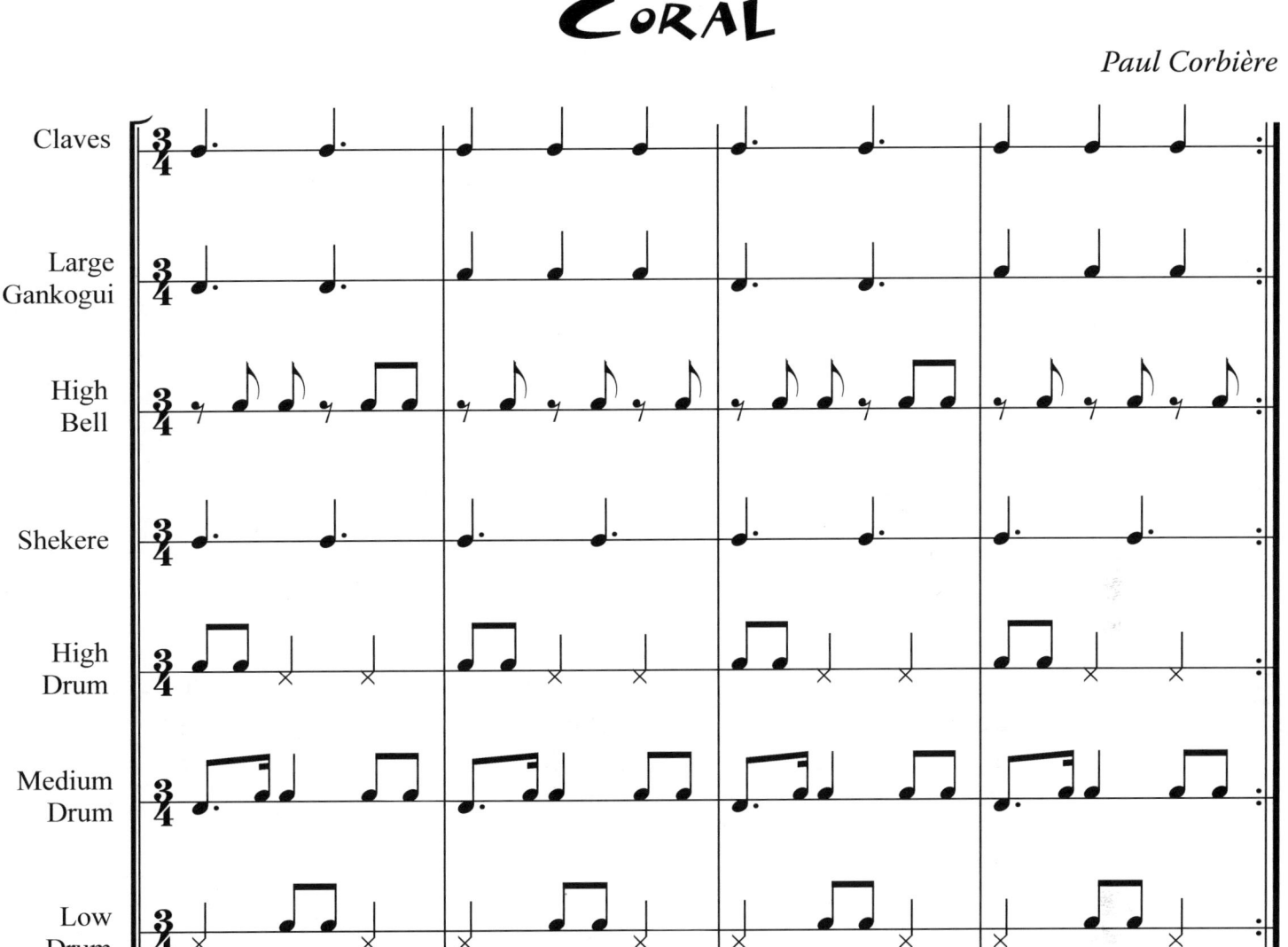

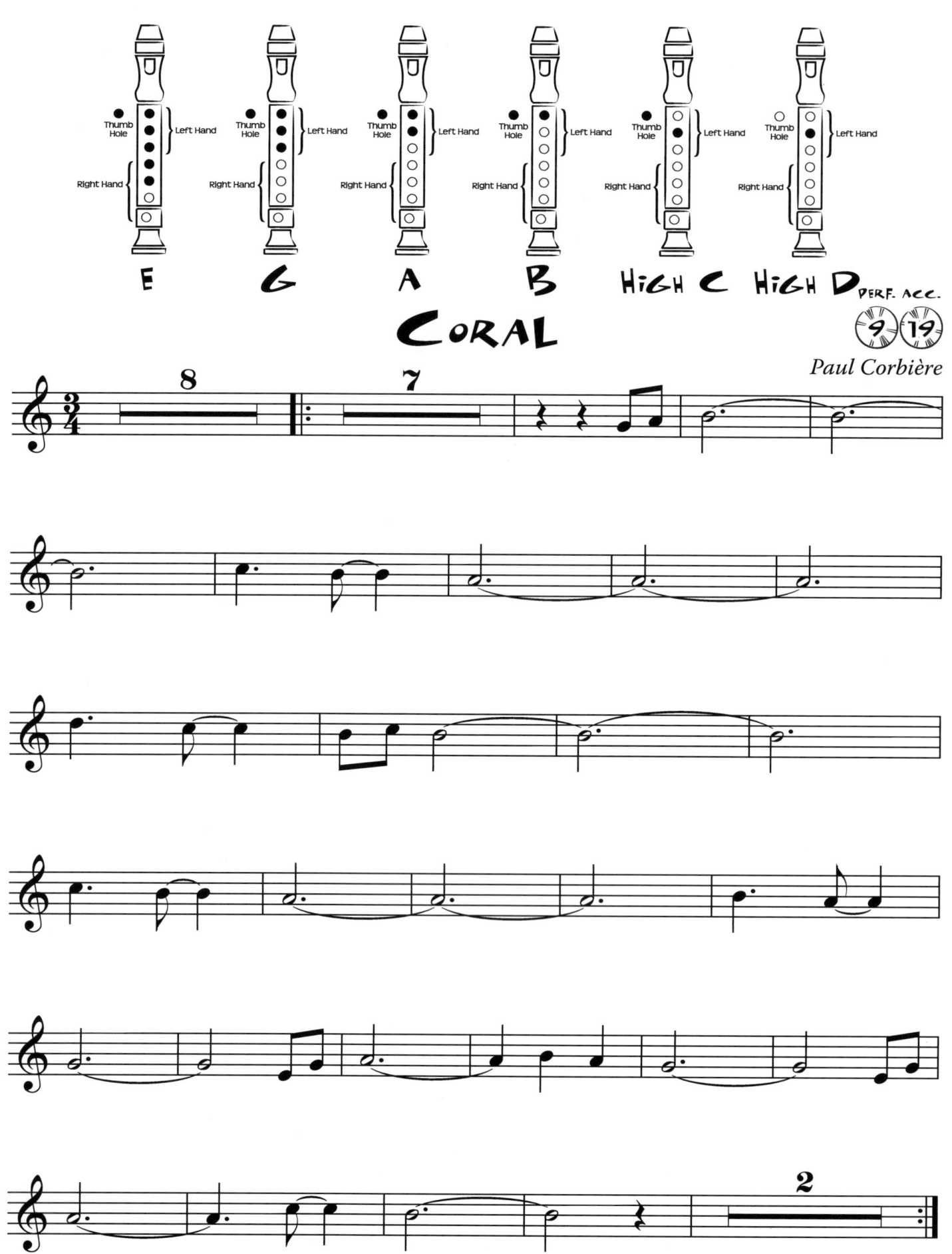

Coral

Paul Corbière

Meet the Composer

Paul Corbière has taught elementary music for more than nineteen years in Florida and in Iowa, where he is currently the K–6 music teacher at Roundy Elementary in Columbus Junction. Paul has been a member of the World Music Drumming teaching staff since 1999 and is a co-founder of the Beat for Peace program, combining World Music Drumming and resiliency research for students with multiple risk factors. Paul has been a featured clinician at many music education association conferences and has conducted multiple residencies with elementary students throughout the United States. Paul is a consultant for *Just Play It! Classroom Harmonica Method*, a blues harmonica curriculum. He is also the author of *Skins, Sticks, and Bars*, a book of drum and xylophone ensembles.

Special Thanks

My wife, Melissa Blum, for her love and continued support of my "Paul-ness."

My family, for their love and support of me, including my sons, Phillip and Matthew Corbière—a couple of "cool monks!" And Grace and Lily Huber for putting up with me—someone has to.

Judy Pine, Robin Walenta, and Steve West of West Music, for their continued support of me.

Will Schmid, for his support of me and because, well, he's a cool dude! (Need I say more?)

John Svec at Minstrel Recording Studios, Iowa City, Iowa, for his expertise in the recording, mastering, and production of the CD.